準備過冬

Sharing the Planet | Non-Fiction Series

Published by Level Learning, INC.

Content Contributors:
Washington Yu Ying PCS™ - Qianyi (Shirley) Zhang, Pearl Zao
He You
Level Learning - Jingyao Qi

Illustrations by: Josh Taira

Leveling classification based on Level Learning standard.
For full description, visit www.levellearning.com

ISBN 978-1-64040-065-8
Traditional Chinese Edition

About Level Learning:

Level Learning provides a literacy focused curriculum specifically designed for K-12 Chinese as a Second Language classrooms. Our program offers 20 levels of specific and detailed objectives, leveled texts and passages, mastery-based online assessment, and analytics to enable data-driven instruction. Level Learning reading curriculum for both literature and informational text emphasize grammar and comprehension skills to help teachers develop confident and independent Chinese language readers. The non-fiction series of books are specifically designed to support our informational text course based on multiple national standards. To learn more about our entire offering, visit www.levellearning.com.

About Washington Yu Ying PCS™:

Washington Yu Ying PCS is a Mandarin English dual language immersion International Baccalaureate (IB) World school. Yu Ying's mission is to inspire and prepare young people to create a better world by challenging them to reach their full potential in a nurturing Chinese/English educational environment. Yu Ying's comprehensive IB, dual immersion curriculum equips students with global competencies for success in the real world. As a leader in immersion education, Yu Ying is determined to advance Chinese language programs and global citizenry education by helping other schools create and strengthen their Chinese programs. For more information, email: products@washingtonyuying.org

冬天就要到了。

在樹下，一隻松鼠在跑來跑去。

這隻松鼠在做什麼呢？

松鼠在找吃的東西。

牠準備過冬了。

在河邊，小青蛙都不見了。

青蛙去哪裡了呢？

青蛙要在家裡睡一整個冬天。

青蛙要準備過冬了。

看天上，一群大雁飛過天空。

這群大雁要去哪裡呢？

大雁要飛到溫暖的地方。

大雁要準備過冬了。

冬天來了，你準備好過冬了嗎？

Glossary

	Pinyin	English Definition
松鼠	sōng shǔ	squirrel
找	zhǎo	to search
準備	zhǔn bèi	to prepare
過冬	guò dōng	to get through winter
河邊	hé biān	river bank
青蛙	qīng wā	frog
睡	shuì	sleep
整個	zhěng gè	entire
大雁	dà yàn	wild geese
天空	tiān kōng	sky
群	qún	flock
溫暖	wēn nuǎn	warm

www.ingramcontent.com/pod-product-compliance
Lightning Source LLC
Chambersburg PA
CBHW041224070526
44584CB00001B/92
* 9 7 8 1 6 4 0 4 0 0 6 5 8 *